The Theory
and
Practice
of Joy

by

Rory Link

Coyote Eye Press
Seattle, Washington

Published in the United States of America by Coyote Eye Press

For information, please contact the publisher:
Coyote Eye Press

Telephone: 206-200-4492
Email:coyoteeyepress@comcast.net

Layout by Jan Nicosia

ISBN: 978-0-9909255-0-7

Printed in the United States of America

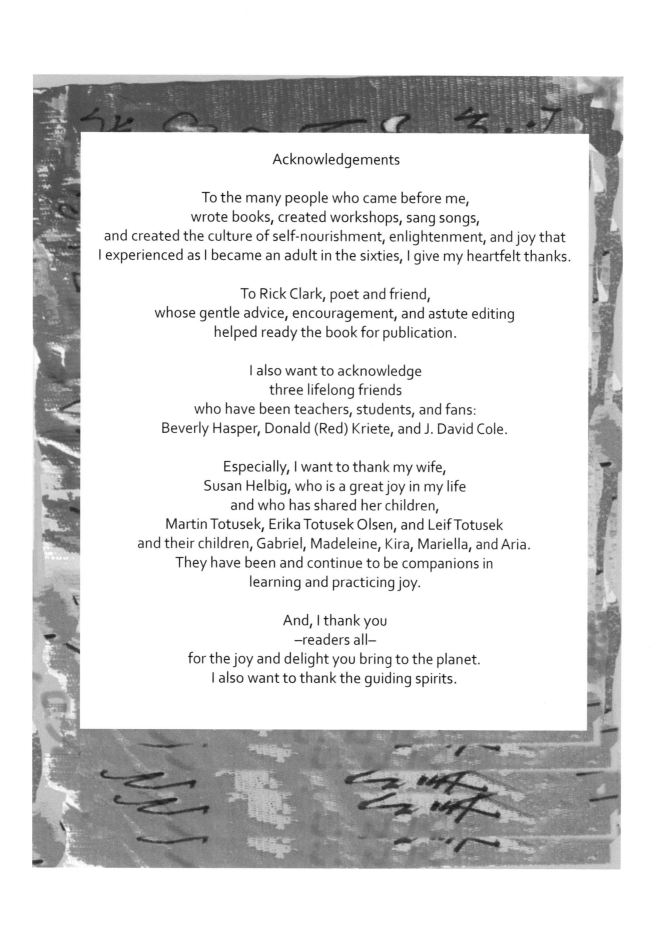

Acknowledgements

To the many people who came before me,
wrote books, created workshops, sang songs,
and created the culture of self-nourishment, enlightenment, and joy that
I experienced as I became an adult in the sixties, I give my heartfelt thanks.

To Rick Clark, poet and friend,
whose gentle advice, encouragement, and astute editing
helped ready the book for publication.

I also want to acknowledge
three lifelong friends
who have been teachers, students, and fans:
Beverly Hasper, Donald (Red) Kriete, and J. David Cole.

Especially, I want to thank my wife,
Susan Helbig, who is a great joy in my life
and who has shared her children,
Martin Totusek, Erika Totusek Olsen, and Leif Totusek
and their children, Gabriel, Madeleine, Kira, Mariella, and Aria.
They have been and continue to be companions in
learning and practicing joy.

And, I thank you
—readers all—
for the joy and delight you bring to the planet.
I also want to thank the guiding spirits.

Rainbow Dancers

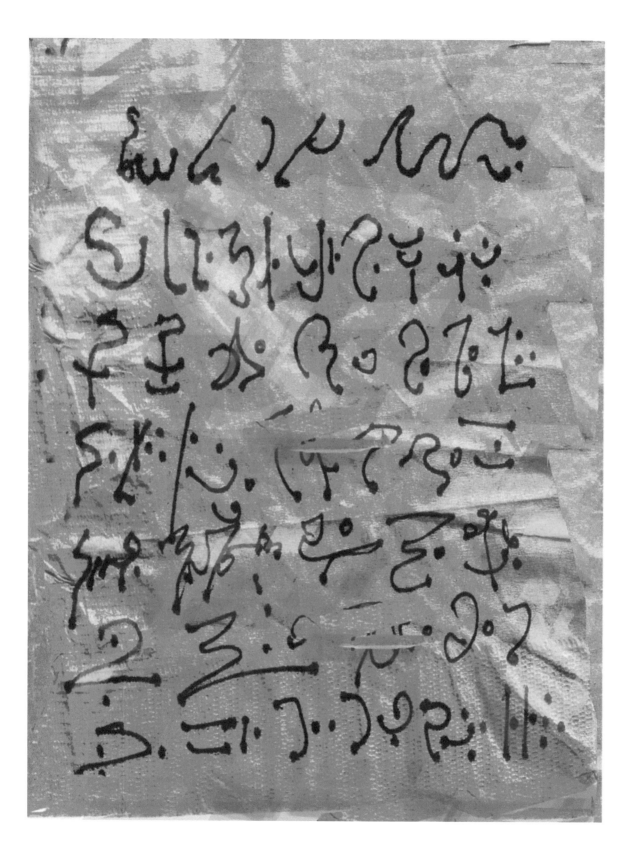

Sunjoy

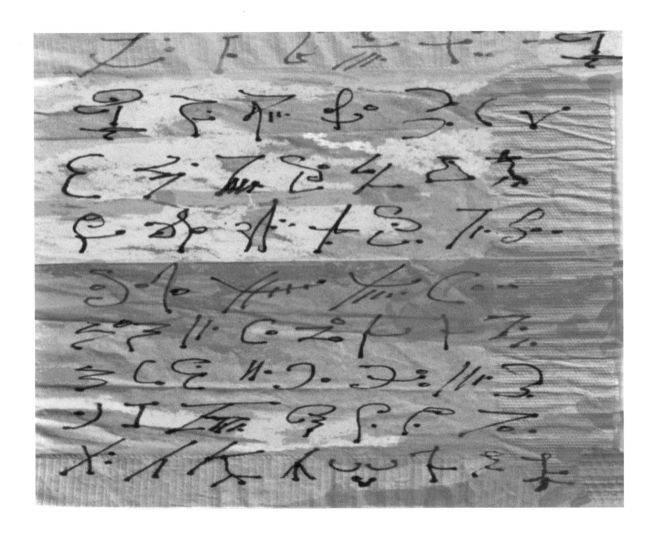

Sand Dune Poetry

The illustrations in this book are original art from my series of excursions into what I call glyphalalia, calligraphy or glyphs in the manner of speaking in tongues (see glossolalia). The glyphs have meaning for me at a subconscious depth. I find them fun, beautiful, and mysterious. Perhaps they will have meaning for you or perhaps be visually appealing. I hope you enjoy them and learn something about yourself in looking at them.

Rory Link

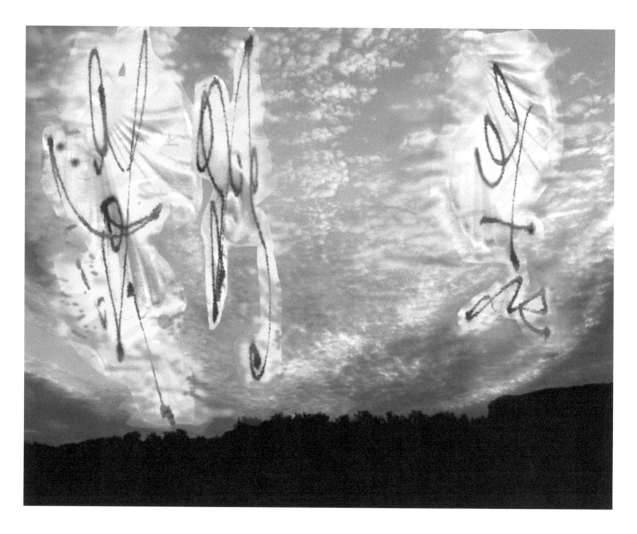

Visitation Of Glyph Angels

Joy is engagement of your energy with the energy of the universe.

Joy is not about following rules,
Nor is it about breaking rules. Enlightenment is a very powerful form of joy,
occurring at the moment all rules and blockages of energy are removed.

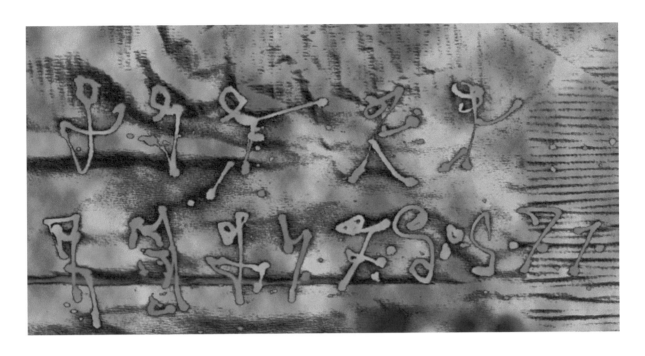

Mall Dancers

Joy is the feeling of energy that spontaneously erupts through you from the bottoms of your feet through the top of your head; it is the energy of the earth moving within the cosmos.

Joy lights the face from within and connects you to the energy of the universe.

Call it god or whatever; it is your felt connection.

Joy is the physical, emotional, and spiritual manifestation of your connection with all that is.

ENJOY.

Affirmation Of Self Identity

I am
I am the consciousness
That asks who I am

I am the consciousness
That perceives myself
And the world around me

I am the sum that is
Greater than all my parts
I am not
      My mind
      My body
      My family
      My job

I am the sum

I am not
      My emotions
      My fears
      My past

I am the sum that is
Greater than all my parts

I am the consciousness
That resides in my soul

I am the love I have
For all in my life

I am the sum that is
Greater than all my parts
I am.

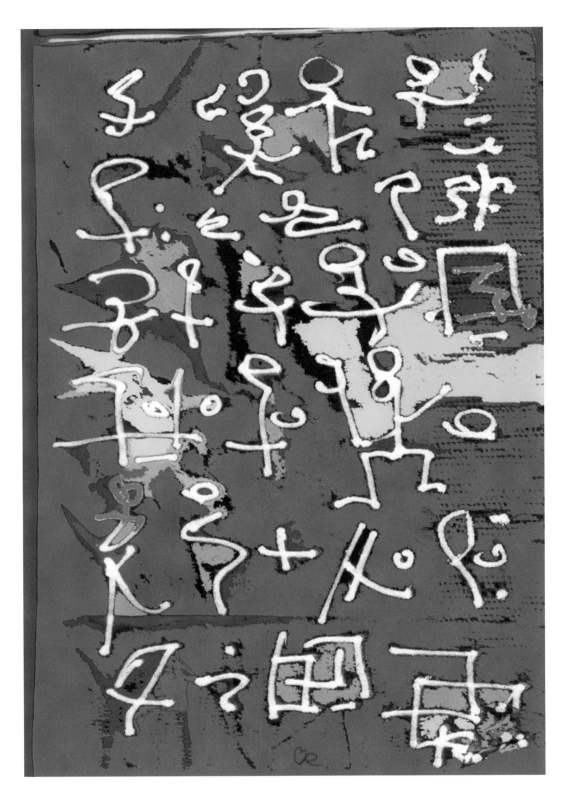

Glyph School

Monks Receiving A Blessing

We live in a paradox of being separate, yet connected. Learn to see where you end and the rest of the world begins—in your body and in your mind. Enjoy yourself. You can perceive your connection to everything and everyone when you are enjoying.

Parade Of Peppers

When negative thoughts persist, choose to think positive thoughts. Speak out loud: "I am not my negative thoughts. I choose to think more positive thoughts. I am all that I am."

Enjoy

A meditation:

Stand or sit comfortably

Close your eyes; take a couple of deep breaths.

Begin chanting the word *enjoy*.

Make your internal voice deep and loud.

Stretch out the word *enjoy* for as long as you can
(about the length of a long slow exhalation or inhalation).

Try vibrating your body tissues with this internal sound. You may find one tone that is more effective for you. When you find your toes vibrating to the sound of *enjoy*, you know you are doing it.

The vibration can relax your muscles, dissolve pain, and change your mood. This meditation can also change the tone of a whole room. Try doing this in a space where people are not smiling. You will see people beginning to smile.

Say   ENJOY . . . . 10 times   (slowly)

        ENJOY . . . .
        ENJOY . . . .
        ENJOY . . . .
        ENJOY . . . .
        ENJOY . . . .
        ENJOY . . . .
        ENJOY . . . .
        ENJOY . . . .
        ENJOY . . . .
        ENJOY . . . .

Saying this mantra silently in a room full of people can lighten the general atmosphere. This can help when you have the blues.

Transdimensional Snowplay

Observe the times when you have more than one emotion. Notice that you tend to choose one or the other. The dominant emotions in your life are your choice.

Acceptance Affirmation

I   Accept
    My life,
    And the lives of others.

I   Accept
    That the world is as it is.

I   Accept
    The changes that we go through.

I   Accept
    That we can and do change the world.

I   Accept
    The world as it will be.

I   Allow
    Myself to accept my own power.

I   Accept
    Responsibility for my actions in the world.

I   Accept
    The slowness of change in the world and in myself.

I am
    The being that
    Allows my body, mind, and soul to accept.

I am
    All the acceptance that I allow.

Kansas 1693

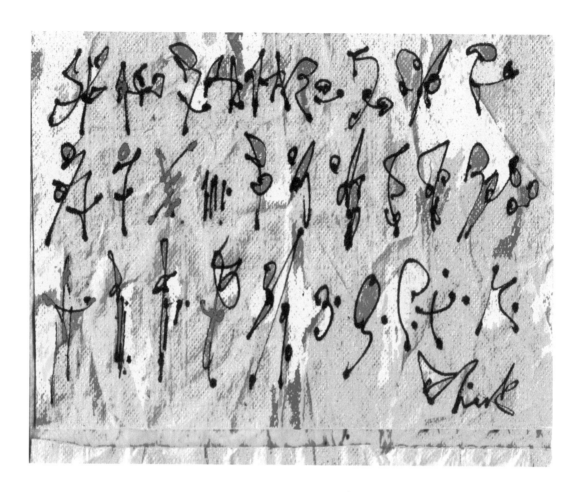

Glyphs Dancing

Learning new things is a way of discovery.

Discovery can often stimulate joy.

When you see someone experiencing joy, let yourself go with the joy.

Remember times when you have experienced joy.
Remember times when you have seen others experiencing joy.

Open yourself to re-experience the joy you remember.

Take time each day to remember happy times.

Seek out affirmations that assist you in creating a positive outlook.
Your attitude is your own. You can choose to be happy.
Spend more time around small children. Observe and feel their joy.

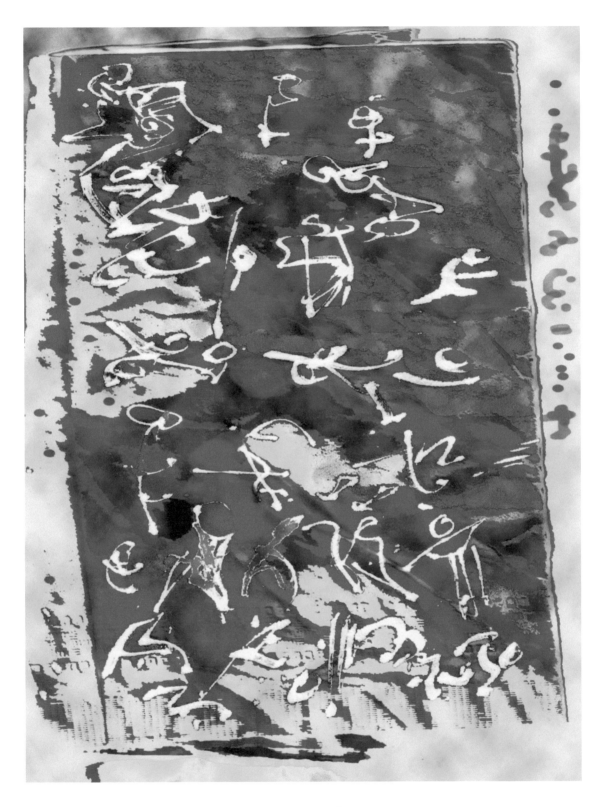

Blufrog Lines

Sluggo's Dream

So often we make small things far more important than they are. See troubles and worries in a larger perspective; they'll have less impact.

Most worrying is circular. If you are worrying about something until the voice of worry is repeating itself, tell that voice to report back when it has new information or a solution to the problem. Be persistent. "Bring me new information, a solution, or at least the beginning of a plan of action." That voice is yours and will follow your direction.

You can program your mind. Sit quietly. Tell yourself that you have the ability to command your mind—the subconscious and unconscious. You can set tasks for those parts. For example:

"I am directing my subconscious to provide me information about the process of becoming more joyful."

You can do this and probably do already: "I'll sleep on it." "Let me think this over." Or "I was wool gathering." These conscious thoughts are usually indications of the need to retrieve subconscious thoughts.

Florasantos

Mosaic At Night

Allow yourself time to retrieve subconscious material. Allow the thoughts to come until useful information flows past your mind's eye. Gently guide your thoughts to the information you need. When solving a complex problem, gently guide your thoughts: "Back to the plumbing, please." Ask gentle questions to guide your thoughts.

Don't be upset if other thoughts or images intrude. Sudden insights can occur in the middle of seemingly unrelated images.

Notice the feeling when an insight blooms in your mind. This feeling is probably joy.

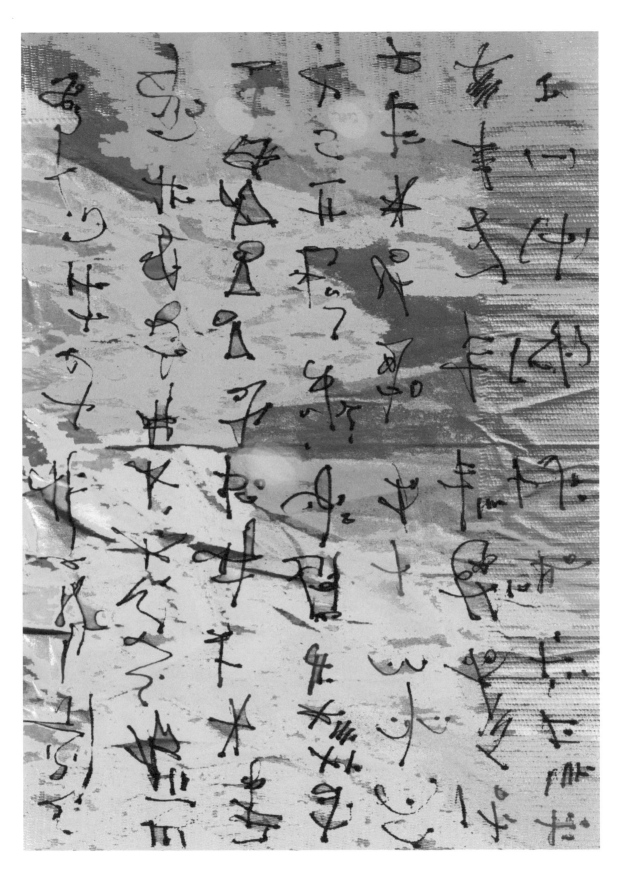

Serpent's Flower

Elephant And The Desert

Agreements

Keep your agreements.
Broken agreements often create guilt and anger within yourself and within the person with whom you have broken the agreement.
If you cannot keep an agreement, renegotiate the agreement.
Make only agreements that you can keep.
This includes being on time, returning borrowed items, and returning telephone calls.

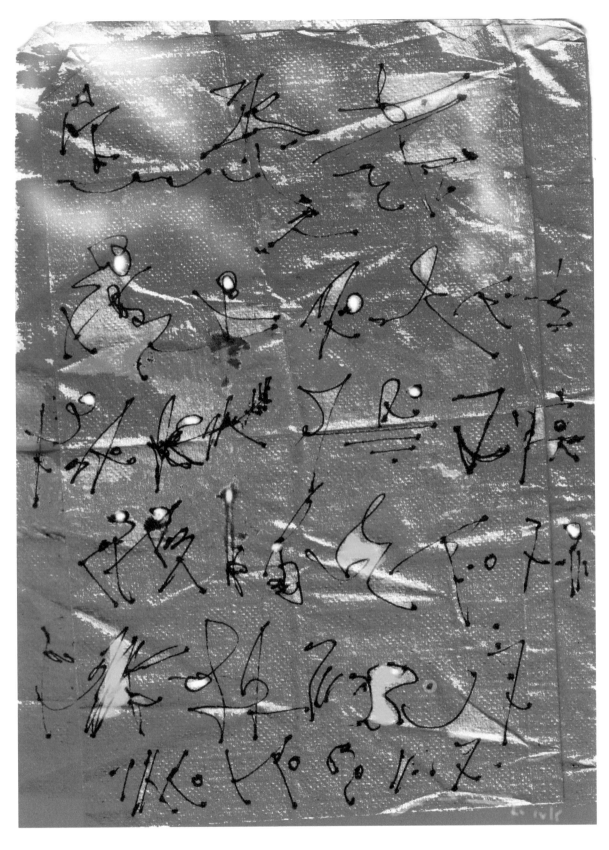

Fishing In The Niche

A Meditation In Practice:

I imagine a dial switch in my mind that I can turn to whatever emotion I want. I often choose to set it at ENJOY or JOY. You can create other positions on the dial, like calm or courage. It takes practice, so try it out. Children seem to find this exercise easy if they are not too upset.

This does not mean you should ignore or suppress other emotions. Rather, it means to let them each have their place and adequate time. If you stay too long in one emotion, it can begin to feel too heavy or flat. Emotions can become habitual. Change emotions if you feel stuck.

When smelling flowers, let them become your whole reality for a second. Breathe in the energy from the flower. Breathe in the essence of their beauty.

When you listen to music, let music enter into your whole body. Imagine a funnel directing the music to your aches or pains.

Give thanks that you are you. Thanks might take the form of saying:

Thank you for creating me as I am.
I give thanks that I am.

You do not have to specify to whom or what you are giving thanks.
If it pleases you, give thanks to a variety of people or deities. It is your internal feeling of thankfulness or gratitude that is important. Your internal sense of self is your connection to the universal force.

Give thanks to yourself for being.
Thank yourself for acknowledging...You.

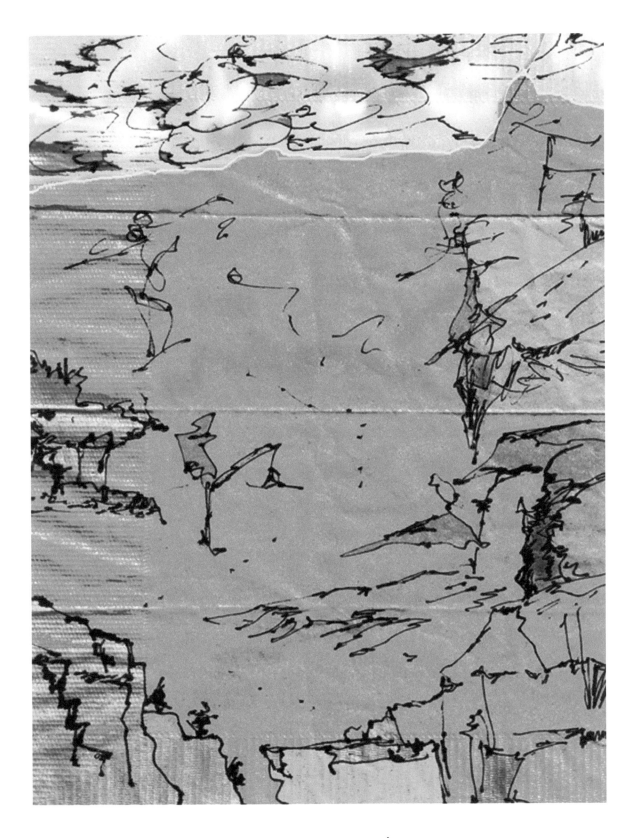

Strangeland

Poly Dancers

FORGIVE

Begin by forgiving yourself. Write on a piece of paper the things that you can forgive about yourself. On the other side of the paper, write down all the people you want to forgive. Try to fill both sides for a few days. Then, burn or recycle the sheets of paper. Even small slights can drain you if not forgiven. Every act of forgiveness makes one feel lighter.

Observe words, particularly the refrain or chorus of your favorite songs—or the ones you habitually sing. Does the meaning enhance your life? Could you choose a more positive song?

Observe your sense of humor. Do you find humor in jokes that hurt or put down other people? These situations may well create tension in you. Think about them. Resolve the tension by meditating on how you feel demeaned by the joke. Notice that you can choose other feelings. The unhappiness of other people is not who you are.

Cultivate other forms of humor that don't harm people. Puns are my favorite form of humor. They stimulate the brain and promote creativity by involving both sides of the brain. Seeing the funny side of difficult situations can help relieve tension without harming people. Making fun of yourself is also a tension reliever.

Glyph Appealing To The Bedrock Of Reality

Pay Attention

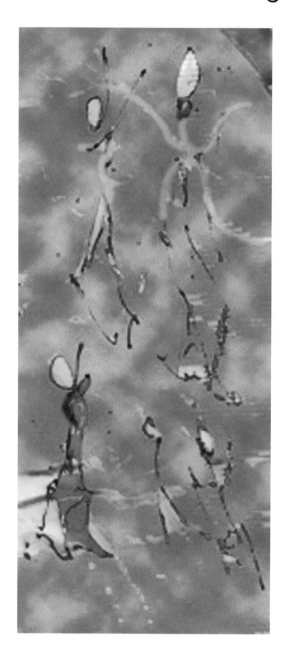

Pay attention
     To your intention,
Pay attention to your life.
The chatter in your mind can really matter
     If it's unkind.
Pay attention to your intention
     Take control of that chatter
     Make it matter in your life.
Ask yourself
     Where does this thought come from?
     Is it really true? What does it prove?
Let compassion be your passion,
     Pay attention to your life.
Let your mind wander,
     Try out new ideas.
You can control
     Its direction
Ask yourself the questions;
     Is this some place
I want to go?
     Is this some thing,
     I need to know?
Pay attention
     To your intention
Pay attention to your life.
Your affection
     Can be your direction.
Let compassion
     Be your passion,
Pay attention
     To your intention
Pay attention to your life...
Become tender
     And surrender
Surrender to your life.
Pay attention
     To your intention
Pay attention to your life.
Pay attention to your life.

Suprise Salad

Surprise yourself with a spontaneous surprise gift to a friend,
a gift that you know he or she wants or needs.
Feel your joy.
Observe theirs.
Random acts of kindness can be an occasion for joy.

Picnic At Pink Rock

Develop rituals that are soothing:

- a candlelit bath with herbal scents
- beating a drum while chanting "enjoy" or nonsense syllables
- singing in the shower
- picking flowers immediately after work
- sharing in your religious or spiritual practices
- drinking a cup of tea in silence

Do not allow rituals to become compulsive. Change rituals now and then. Use ritual as a form of play.

Innerchild At The Beach

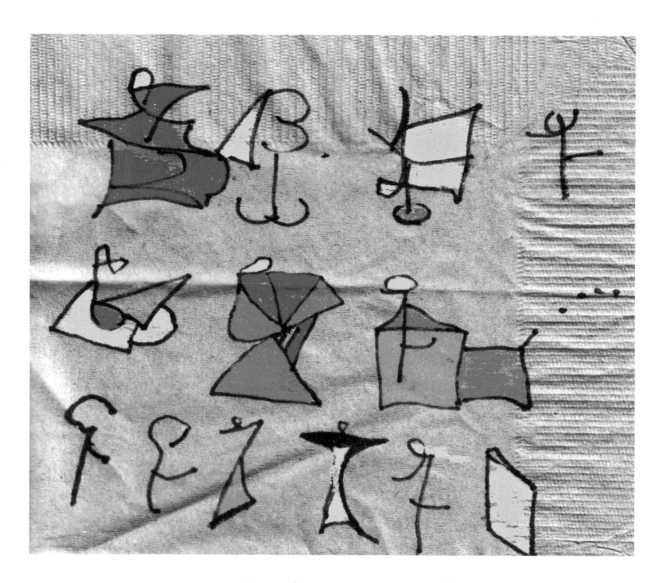

Transforming The Blessings

Greet the Sun in Thankfulness:
When you first see the sun each day, stand erect and bask in its rays. Silently or out loud say:
"Thank you, Sun, for your warmth, your light."
Close your eyes and imagine or feel yourself filling with light.
"Thank you, Sun, for filling me with light."

Thank Mother Earth for giving you a home.
Feel your connection to her gravity.
Feel your sense of belonging.

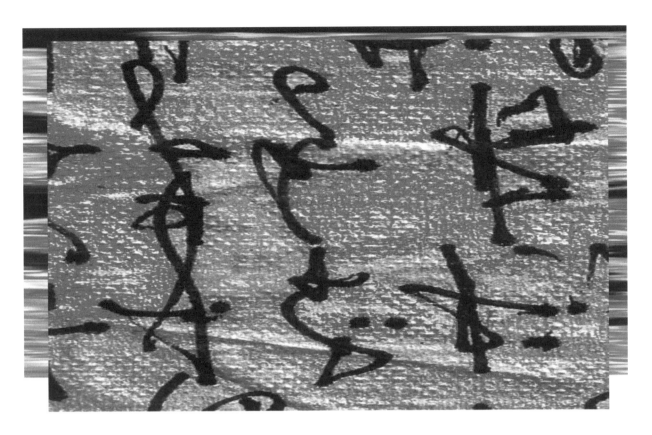

Dancing The Animals

Be kind. The mere act of kindness can create a subtle glow of well-being. It can help you feel grateful about your ability to be kind.

Kindness is its own reward.

Be kind to yourself.

Be kind to your neighbors.

Be kind to your family.

Be kind to your friends.

Be kind to our Earth.

Sun Healing Meditation:

Sit in the sun with your eyes closed. Imagine your body filling up with the golden light of the sun. Breathe the light into all parts of your body.

Notice how good it feels.
Notice your thoughts.

Breathe in the golden light of the sun until you can feel it shining out of you.

You can do this at anytime, even in the middle of the night. Just imagine golden light coming into the soles of your feet, into the top of your head, or through your upraised hands until it fills you up.

How good it feels!
How good it is.

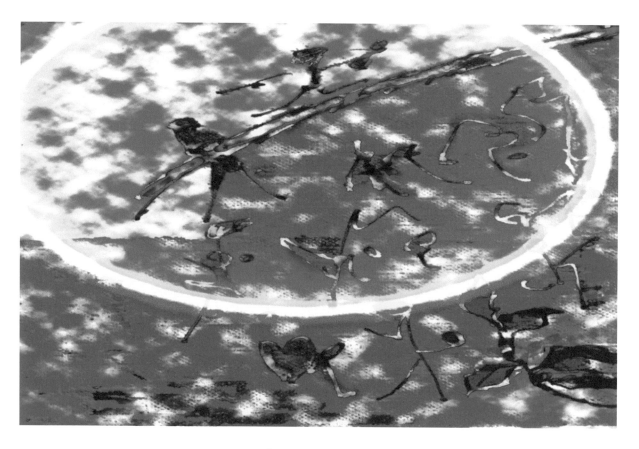

Balance Dance

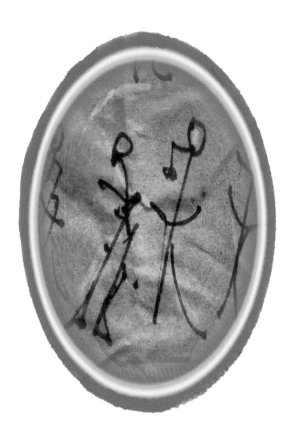

Sundogs Dancing On The Lawn

Self talk:

We all talk to ourselves,
     Is it positive?
     Is it practical?
     Is it negative?
     Is it critical?

We can control this self-talk. When we are being negative or criticizing others or ourselves, we can gently redirect our thoughts toward solutions, ideas to make things work better, or corrective measures.

We can use this critical energy to create positive changes.
Sometimes we need to communicate some of these thoughts to others. Letters to the editor, comments on a blog, Twitter, online forums—the avenues for self expression are many.

Judgment:

Often, we need to use judgment. Judgment is necessary for making decisions. We need to use good judgment in many situations. Idly judging those around us, people on the street, etc., in a negative way can be destructive. These negative judgments serve no purpose other than to give us a grim view of life. Making negative judgments all day makes our days gray and unhappy.

Resist the urge to negatively judge others; it makes our face look bad and does not help anything. Unneeded judgment can harm us, our bodies, and the people we are judging. This is self-talk that we do not need.

Green Cat Digs The Blues

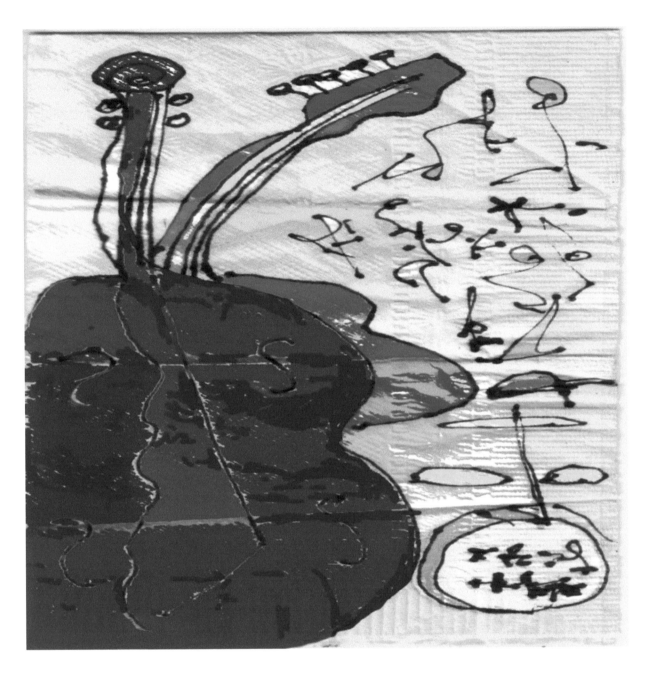

Jazz

Consider your goals: Do you have goals that you've held onto for years? Even though you know you will never achieve those goals? Was it ever achievable? Often we have unrealized goals from our childhood or youth that have turned into negative evaluations of ourselves. We may even hold them unconsciously. Try to uncover them. Change them to realistic goals or delete them. You will feel relief.

Pink Bliss

Investigate self-help books. Look for "Aha!" moments, epiphanies of understanding. Practice affirmations that target some of your problems.

As you read books, articles or even fortune cookies, observe those that resonate with your life. Observe the feeling of resonance. That feeling is the beginning of joy. It's trying to break through.

Resonance is a connection to your perceptions. You can actually feel it. Whether this resonance is positive or negative, you can use it to understand yourself and find a way to create a positive experience.

Sometimes, watching television can create a feeling of joy. Take note of what creates joy or a feeling of connection. Kitten pictures on the Internet seem to bring millions of people joy. Explore Internet options if you can.

Buckskin Fuschia

Your Book of Joy

Collect writings that makes you feel good in a folder or notebook: photos, poems, words from a song, affirmations. Call it your Book of Joy. Even write down songs to play on your music system.

Alternatively, collect, mementoes, photos, rocks, etc., from happy times or treasures whose intrinsic beauty give you joy and keep them in a box.

Create a ritual using small precious objects to count your blessings.

Create your own methods for feeling joy. You probably already have.

> Make it conscious.
> Make it a practice.

Fuschia

Surrender. Give up. Accept the fact that you're not going to solve all the world's problems. You're not going to become a star on Broadway or a sports hero over-night. By accepting that some goals are out of reach, you create a space for new goals that you can reach. You'll find space to look at the goals that you've reached, perhaps not grandiose goals, but goals reached, never the less.

You've achieved a great deal to reach this point in your life. You care about yourself, and you're willing to learn. For example, you have reached the goal of reading. What an important achievement. Think about it! Reading is a window to the thoughts of the world.

Forgive yourself for the goals you have not reached.
Forgive yourself for the times you have been sad or negative or depressed.
Forgive yourself for having had bad, mean, or evil thoughts too. Tell them (the thoughts) they are not needed and are not helpful. Tell them to go away.
Yes, you can talk to thoughts. Thoughts talk to you.
Tell your mind to give you happier or at least more useful thoughts.

Give yourself a break.
Give yourself another chance.
Give yourself congratulations and affirmations.
Give yourself… You.

Everything that is, has been, or will be, contributes to the uniqueness that is you. You are unique and important to the wholeness of the universe.

Coyote Sending Glyphs To Cloud Spirit

Cherish your:

loved ones
memories
friends
treasures
pets.

Cherish the cave woman who is your ancestress.
Cherish all the good times you've had.
Cherish the joy you have had with friends and loved ones
        who have passed on.
Cherish each day as if it were the first sunny day of spring.

Whale Dreams

Be grateful:
        for what you have,
        for your friends,
        for the uniqueness that is you,
        for the joys you have, and
        for the future and the past.

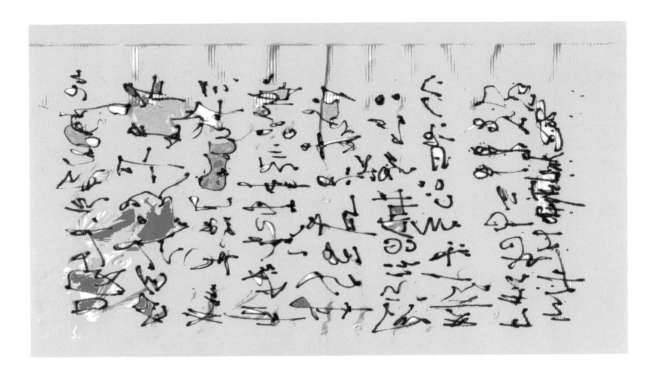

Who's Green

Silly

My granddaughter and I have an agreement: "There's nothing wrong with being silly." If you really think about it, much of our world is just plain silly. It's silly that it sells too. What could be sillier than gold-plated water faucets?

We all have times when something struck us as so silly that we giggle uncontrollably. Remember? Didn't that feel good?

Laughter:

Watch a comedy. Read funny stories.
If something strikes you as funny, really laugh.
Tell a joke now and then.
Take time to listen to a joke.

Engage:

Have you ever noticed how good you feel when talking to a friend about something you both find exciting?

That's engagement.

When you're working on a project that you are totally committed to, you feel engaged. Your sense of self is about the energy you feel flowing through you to the friend or project. Worries, pains, and sorrows disappear; there is only the connection.

Being present to the energy flowing through yourself is engagement. Positive engagement, or life-affirming energy, produces the sensation of joy, and you can feel the energy coming back to you and through you.

Be in the present—feel this moment. Being in the present is an act of joy. Joy is your connection to all there is. It is yours to feel, yours to become.

Find your joy—share your joy.

Enjoy.

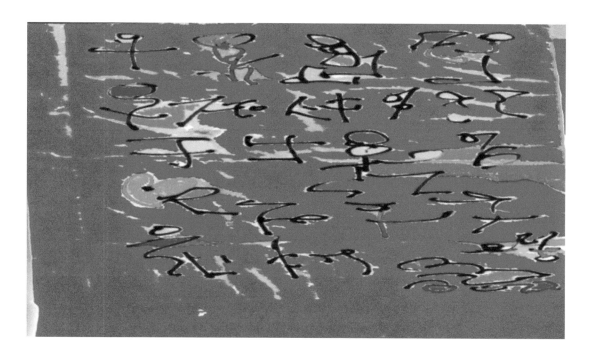

Poppy Rhythm

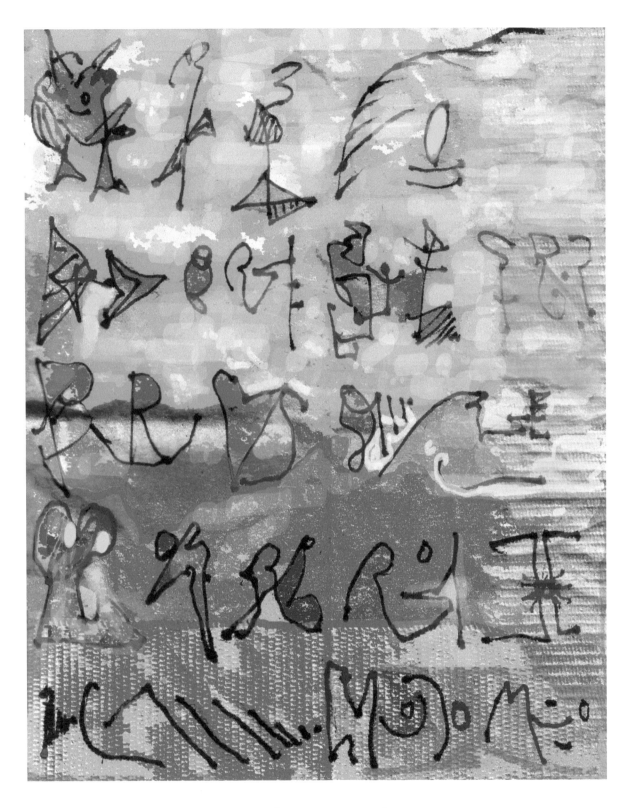

Carnival Monday

Have fun, for the fun of it.

Allow your inner child to emerge playfully in appropriate ways:

- Break into a little dance step now and then when walking.
- Relearn how to skip.
- Sing a childhood song now and then at the top of your voice.
- Sometimes just yell out loud for no reason at all.
- Smile at people you meet on the street; they are likely to smile back.
- Pick up garbage on the street when walking and deposit it in a trashcan. Others might see you do it and emulate you.
- Check out a garage sale. You may find a treasure or a memory.

For example, I recently found an Alan Watts book I read in my twenties. It brought back memories and a new appreciation of his wisdom. I also saw a toy that was very similar to one I had as a child; it brought back good memories. You may also find something you need, like a tool or a piece of furniture that is just what you were looking for. Buying at garage sales is a fun way to recycle. You may be surprised in a joyous way. You may meet wonderful people.

When you see people that make you feel sad because their lives are obviously difficult and unhappy, chant enjoy ten times. You'll feel better, and so will they.

    You are not their problems.

    They are not their problems.   .

They are an expression of the universe, the soul that is creating their world. This does not mean you should not have compassion. You can do more for others if you do not become attached to negative emotions—sadness, anger, despair, guilt, etc. A joyous heart will find a better way. Volunteering is a good way to find joy even in sad situations.

Teach:
  We all know something.
  We all learn new things.
Share:
  your joy,
  a chocolate bar,
  a favorite place,
  memories of a mutual loved one.

Share the wisdom you have acquired.
Share your time.
Take time to call friends or relatives, for no reason except to spend time with them.

Glyph Teaching The Clouds How To Sing

Visit those you love and those who love you.
Visit shut-ins and people who are lonely.
Get to know your neighbors.

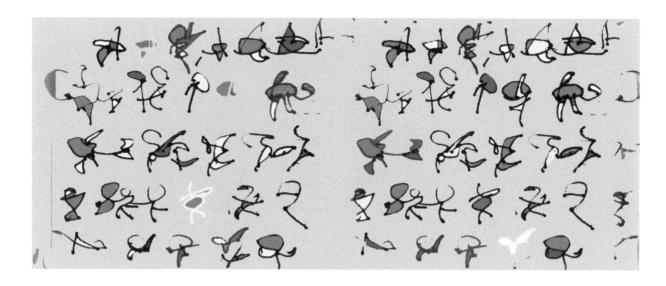

Two Party Glyphs

Exercise:
Find an exercise program that makes you feel good.
Buy a dog to walk. Or borrow a dog from a friend.
A dog's joy in being with you is infectious.
Go for walks just to see what is in your neighborhood.
Visit some other neighborhood for a walk.
Go for a walk in the country or on a beach.

Go dancing. Dance around your living room. Make a joyous noise.
You are not required to be a great dancer, great singer, or musician to experience joy. Let yourself express...You.

Participate:

Join a club or find a charity that needs your help. Organize your neighborhood. Take part in the life around you. Find a circle of like-minded friends to meet on a regular basis. Go to a local play. Volunteer somewhere. Helping or becoming part of a project can be very rewarding.

Find a hobby that exercises your body and your mind. Gardening is great for both mind and body. There are many activities that bring pleasure to our mind, body, and spirit, that bring pleasure to others, creating a feedback loop of pleasure. Try it. You will like it.

Leviathan On The Prairie

Surrender to your life, whatever it is. Do the best at living your life that you can. When you surrender to your life you can see it for what it is without deceiving yourself or making excuses. If you need to, change your life to be happy. Surrender to those changes. You change all the time. You can change for the better. Surrender to the idea that you can find happiness as... You!

Yeah, You! You deserve to be happy, and so does everyone else.

You are the "I" of yourself.
Enjoy Yourself.

Bear Spirit In The Clouds

Observe nature. Look at clouds.
Watch them change.
Can you see a pattern? Is it you finding shapes or is it the clouds? Are these pictures a message to you from your deeper self?
They may be memories or thoughts to ponder. You decide. Enjoy them, in any case.

Imagination:

Exercise it. It is a muscle that needs a workout now and then. Make your imagination positive.

Imagine a day when everything goes right.
Imagine a sunny day when you can play or work outside.
Imagine being happy.
Imagine being content.
Imagine creating something.
Imagine being generous, without any thought of being paid back.
Imagine being deeply in touch with yourself.
Imagine being happy with yourself as you are.
Imagine being able to create joy in others.

Daydream a little. Think of something you would like to do.
Take a nap and dream a little as you fall asleep.

Use your imagination to create. Take up a creative hobby, make music, draw or paint.
Buy some clay and make little figures.
Do this for you. Show your efforts to others only if you want to. Enjoy the process of
learning what the medium can be encouraged to do. Explore.

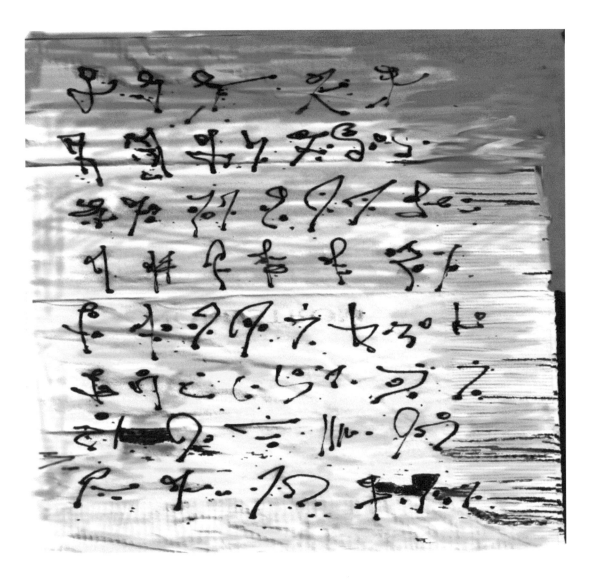

Noordancers

Sands Of Joy

Become a Pillar of Light

Stand relaxed. Take a few deep breaths. Close your eyes. Imagine that you are a pillar of light that extends into the earth and out to the sky. Breathe. Feel the glow. Feel yourself pulsing as light.

Choose a Power Animal

A Power Animal is a spirit animal that you would like to invite to be your friend, guide, teacher, etc. Obtain an image of this animal. Research the animal in science and myth. Make up your own myths if need be.

See what happens.

Don't be too serious, and don't make a religion out of this. Just enjoy having a real imaginary ally that you can talk to, look for, and come to know. Talk to it—you will find that it has a personality. Ask it to be your helper.

Day at the Beach

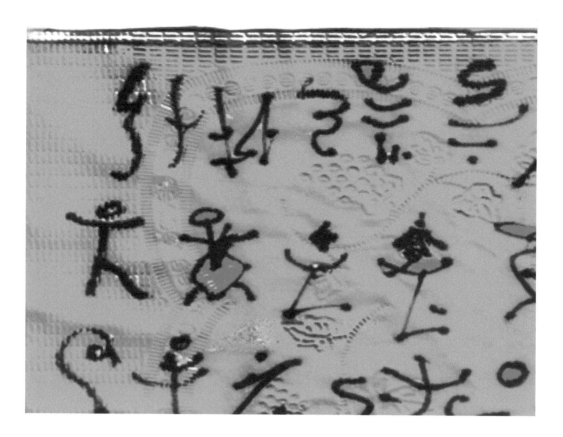

Diamond Jazz

Glossolalia:

Glossolalia is an ancient practice, apparently as old as human speech, perhaps older. Speaking a nonexistent language composed of sounds with no specific meaning, shamanic peoples throughout the ages have invited spirits into their lives and rituals. Some charismatic Christians and people of other religions also practice glossolalia. It can be fun and entertaining, bringing about insights of an unexpected nature. I encourage you to use glossolalia to invite the spirit of joy into your life.

Try it out. If you enjoy it, do it; otherwise, let it be. We don't need to do everything. We need to do what brings us joy. Not all that people do is for everybody. There are many enjoyable solitary pursuits. Look for them. They may be in your past, such as a sport from high school.

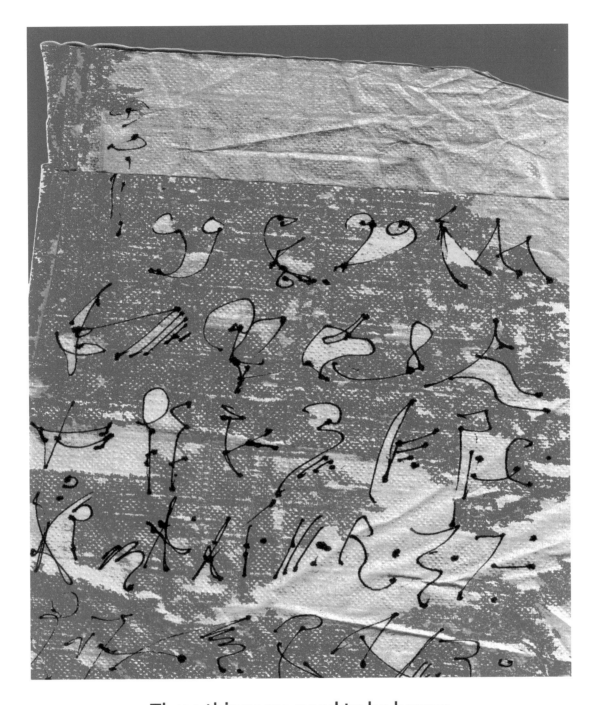

Three things we need to be happy
(beyond food and shelter):
Love, someone to love
and the ability to love our self.

Loving ourself is the key:
for then we're free to love others.

Enjoy Your Life

It is up to you to decide what makes you happy.
Joy is yours if you decide to partake.
Enjoy.

Art and Meditation

I am fortunate to have had a secure and loving childhood that provided so many wonderful experiences. I began meditating as a child of about eight. I lived near Mount Spokane and had free range of nearby Deadman's Creek. While fishing in the creek with a pole made from a maple branch and patiently waiting for fish to bite, I would find myself focusing on a small whirlpool. Without thinking, I began to notice my thoughts. I tried to just observe those thoughts as I was attempting to catch a fish. What I caught, as well as fish, was the ability to watch my mind without attachment.

I wrote poetry in high school, often as a form of meditation. I studied philosophy at Washington State University in eastern Washington, and a variety of liberal arts at the University of Washington. I continued my interest in the mind, reading popular psychology and books that were often pressed on me by my friends. Too late to be a Beatnik and too early to be a Hippie, I nevertheless eventually found myself living a bohemian lifestyle in the mid-1960s on the shores of Seattle's Lake Union. I began drawing and painting, practicing yoga, meditating, and studying Zen and other eastern practices. Painting and poetry became my preferred form of meditation. Consciousness expansion and developing a vital internal life were priorities for me, as was developing a spiritual path.

In 1966, I had a revelation: I would no longer take a job unless I enjoyed it. The very next job lasted two days. My world opened up when I found a job with Al Hansen, a commercial sculptor making brass and copper trees, plastic trees, and other "abstract" pieces. If not technically 'fine art", Al's art was beautiful. I worked with him for nearly 10 years, learning much in the process. I gathered more art skills from other artists, friends, books, observation, and practice. I continued to read voraciously and wrote poetry often.

Somewhere in this journey, I began to find joy. Many experiences, wonderful friends, books, conversations, and ideas pulled me into living life in a joyous manner. I eventually came to understand that joy is a goal, a path, and a way to cope with an imperfect and often harsh or unjust world. As a worthy pursuit, I found that cultivating joy includes practicing peace, love, and understanding.

In 1968, though my ongoing practice, a spirit guide entered my life. She is a spirit venerated by the Salish people, including members of the Swinomish Indian Tribal Community, who believe that she is the spirit of abundance. Ever since she "chose" me and I eventually accepted her, she continues to bring an abundance of everything I need or desire, in addition to leading me into my forty-year practice of many forms of Shamanism.

I have been an active energetic healer for over fifteen years and, on a daily basis, I continue to meditate, practice shamanism, write, and create in many media.

Photo by Jill Sontesby

CPSIA information can be obtained
at www.ICGtesting.com
Printed in the USA
LVHW07n1538240418
574610LV00001BC/1/P